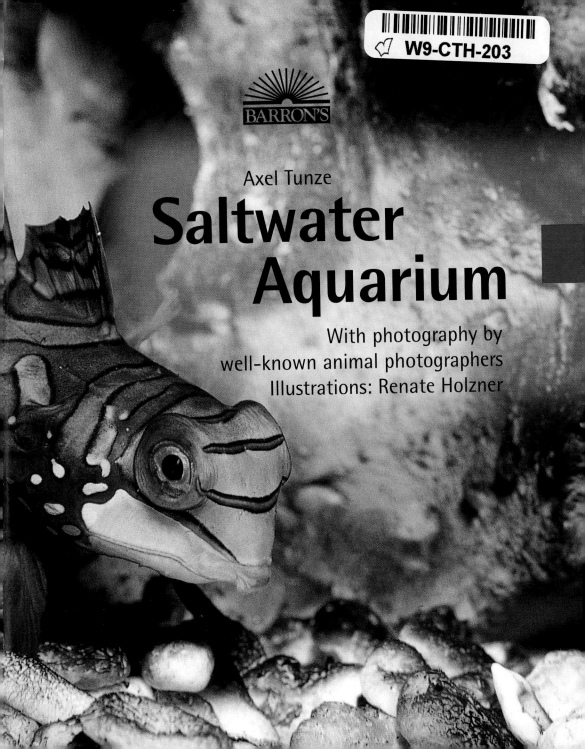

BARRON'S

Axel Tunze

Saltwater Aquarium

With photography by
well-known animal photographers
Illustrations: Renate Holzner

2 CONTENTS

TYPICAL SALTWATER AQUARIUM

- Brilliantly hued fish and fantastically shaped corals.

- Varied and colorful shrimp, crabs, mollusks, and starfish.

- A fascinating ecological community of fish and invertebrates.

- A natural humidifier to improve the climate in your home.

- Tranquility and beauty by day or by night.

The typical marine aquarium recreates one of the world's most fascinating habitats, home to an abundance of species—the tropical coral reef. Here, among higher algae that are relatives of freshwater plants, dwell strikingly colored fish, as well as invertebrates such as corals, crabs, shrimp, mollusks, starfish, and sea urchins.

In the aquarium as well, fish and invertebrates form a unique ecosystem, offering the observer a wide variety of intriguing behavior patterns. Orange-and-white-banded clownfish make their home among the tentacles of a sea anemone; corals obtain nutrients from photosynthetic products of algae living in their tissues. Cleaner shrimp remove unwelcome parasites from the bodies of fish. And a final oddity—the male seahorse that broods and gives birth to the young.

FACTORS TO CONSIDER

1 The initial cost of outfitting a saltwater aquarium is relatively high, because of the considerable technical equipment needed and the required large capacity of the aquarium itself (about 50 gallons [190 L] is the recommended minimum size).

2 Consider also the ongoing costs. Large aquariums use a great deal of electricity for lighting, filtration, and heating. Inadequate aquarium equipment can markedly increase these costs.

3 A thorough understanding of aquarium technology and proper aquarium management is essential.

4 If the saltwater aquarium is properly planned and equipped and the keeper is knowledgeable and experienced, the amount of time required to care for a saltwater aquarium is about the same as for a freshwater aquarium.

5 You should enjoy observing your aquarium inhabitants. If you're primarily interested in the aquarium's decorative value, however, it's advisable to rely on an aquarium maintenance service for routine care.

6 When you travel, you will need a reliable person to care for your aquarium in your absence.

7 Be sure that the location where you plan to install the aquarium is strong enough to support its weight. When in doubt, consult a builder or your landlord.

8 A saltwater aquarium presents almost no risk to persons with allergies. In fact, it can even help in the management of skin and respiratory problems, because the saltwater vapors improve the indoor climate.

9 Keep in mind that a properly managed aquarium can thrive for 10 years or more. Marine fish can live to be 10 to 15 years old.

Comparison with a Freshwater Aquarium

In contrast to a freshwater aquarium, a saltwater aquarium may include not only fish and algae, but also corals and other invertebrates. Invertebrates place high demands on the quality of the aquarium water, and therefore the outlay for aquarium equipment is greater than for a freshwater aquarium. Furthermore, because the marine aquarium hosts a greater variety of species, more attention must be paid to the compatibility of the various animals and plants; this is essential for creating a stable ecosystem within the aquarium. However, a saltwater aquarium that is carefully planned and properly equipped will be just as easy to maintain as a freshwater aquarium.

SELECTING THE AQUARIUM INHABITANTS

Fish, algae, corals, starfish, crabs, shrimp: The variety of species in the saltwater aquarium is vast. Therefore, before making a purchase the aquarium hobbyist must learn all about the needs of the various species and the appropriate interaction between animals and plants.

The Marine Aquarium Ecosystem

In setting up a saltwater aquarium, the compatibility of fish, invertebrates, and higher algae is extremely important. An ecological equilibrium will develop in the aquarium only if the stock of animals and plants is carefully coordinated. Many species serve an ecological function in the aquarium. For example, higher algae are not merely decorative; they serve primarily as a source of food for fish, such as surgeonfish, which in turn check the rapid growth of these algae. Blennies and gobies devour the filamentous algae that are unwelcome in an aquarium. Therefore, when choosing inhabitants for your aquarium, you should consider not only how attractive a species is, but also its ecological benefits. Improper selection or overstocking can cause the water to become loaded with harmful substances (for example, animal wastes and nitrates). If you set up your aquarium as an ecosystem, you will not only learn about interesting life forms, but also achieve better water quality. For suggestions for stocking your aquarium properly, see pages 28–29.

Tropical coral reefs display a fascinating variety of brilliantly colored creatures.

Shopping for an Aquarium

Pet stores carry fish, algae, corals, and other invertebrates. Most of the available species are either imported from their native lands or bred in captivity (see TIP, page 17). A responsible dealer will be able to show you an active aquarium that has been maintained successfully—with the same stock—for at least one year.

Keep these points in mind as you shop:

✔ Before you purchase animals and plants, the aquarium must be completely set up with all the necessary equipment (see page 31).

✔ The seawater must be allowed to stand in the aquarium for a few days (see *Aquarium Installation,* page 39) before the first inhabitants can be introduced.

✔ Stock the aquarium with at least 30 percent live rock (natural reef rock, inhabited by algae, sponges, small crustaceans, and snails; see page 39), algae, and corals before you introduce the fish.

Selecting Animals and Plants

Fish: Because most of the fish sold in pet stores are imported directly from their native habitats, they must first become accustomed to living in an aquarium. Fish that have become

Checklist
Shopping

1 Before you buy animals and plants, the aquarium must be completely set up with all the necessary equipment. The seawater must be allowed to stand for a few days in advance (see page 39).

2 To ensure that your first experience with keeping an aquarium does not end in unnecessary loss of living creatures, be sure to purchase only hardy species and choose compatible animals and plants (see pages 28–29).

3 Inquire about the length of the acclimation period at the pet store (four weeks) and about individual feeding requirements.

4 Do not accept fish that are infested with parasites. There should be no white spots or flecks on the skin.

5 Corals should be fully opened at the time of purchase.

6 Use a quarantine aquarium for all new fish.

acclimated at the pet store may cost more, but they are less susceptible to diseases. This acclimation period should last about four weeks.

What to look for when purchasing fish:
✔ The fish must be well nourished, the body rounded and full. Fish that are thin will have difficulty with the transfer to your aquarium.
✔ Ask the dealer to show you that the fish will eat (frozen) food, and purchase an initial supply of the food they are accustomed to eating.
✔ The fish must be free of parasites; inspect for tell-tale white spots or flecks on the body and fins. A fish that scratches its skin against rocks and corals may also carry parasites (see page 50).
✔ Choose only fish that are appropriate for the size of your aquarium.
✔ Purchase young fish, as they will adjust more readily to life in an aquarium than older fish.
✔ Combine only compatible species, and be sure the number of fish you buy is appropriate for the capacity of your aquarium (see *HOW-TO: Stock the Aquarium*, pages 28–29).

Corals should be fully opened at the time of purchase. Ask the dealer about the coral's requirements for light, nutrients, water flow, and water quality. Note where the corals are located in the pet store aquarium, and imitate this when you install them in your own aquarium.

Shrimp, crabs, mollusks, sea urchins, and other invertebrates are specialists when it comes to food. Find out exactly what each individual species requires. Don't place starfish in a newly established aquarium or an aquarium with mollusks.

Higher algae can be purchased as small plants. If you want to maintain a relatively large amount of algae in your aquarium, you should minimize the number of algae-eating fish you select.

Transporting the Fish

The pet store staff will pack fish and invertebrates in plastic bags with seawater. If the creatures are healthy, they will be safe for several hours at a temperature of 68–77°F (20–25°C). Because the transport period is stressful, however, you should keep the trip home as brief as possible. To maintain a constant temperature, place the bags in an insulated container or wrap them in a blanket. If the marine animals are healthy and have already had an acclimation period at the pet store, they can be introduced into the aquarium (see page 40).

Note: Cautious aquarium keepers place newly acquired specimens in a separate quarantine aquarium for a few weeks, to prevent the spread of any diseases to creatures already living in the aquarium. Many diseases take a while to manifest themselves.

An established saltwater aquarium, complete with interesting corals and vivid fish, is a captivating sight.

Animals and Plants in the Marine Aquarium

On the following pages are profiles of various marine animals and plants that are easy to care for and compatible with one another.

All of these species require water temperatures of 75–82°F (24–28°C).

Size: The size given is the average size that specimens will attain in an 80-gallon (300-L) aquarium. In the wild, the size of individual creatures may vary from those observed in captivity.

Compatibility: Listed here are special characteristics that must be taken into account when combining species in the saltwater aquarium community. Three concrete examples of how to build a workable ecosystem are described under *HOW-TO: Stock the Aquarium* (see pages 28–29).

The Green Chromis (Chromis viridis), a schooling fish, looks green or blue depending on how the light falls.

Marine Aquarium Fish

If the aquarium size permits, fish are best kept in pairs. This corresponds more closely to the natural behavior patterns of many species than keeping a single specimen. Living in pairs increases the life expectancy of many fish. Exceptions are very dominant fish species, such as the surgeonfish; it's better to keep only one of these in a small aquarium, where territorial disputes are unavoidable.

Clown Anemonefish, True Percula
Amphiprion percula (see photo, page 15)
   Family: Damselfish (Pomacentridae)
   Size: 2–3 inches (5–8 cm).
   Care: Keep as a pair, together with a sea anemone (see page 22); the fish live among its tentacles in a symbiotic relationship. Stock the aquarium with one small and one large specimen, because all the fish are male at birth and only the larger ones later become female.
   Diet: Small crustaceans (also frozen food).
   Compatibility: Peaceful toward other fish, except when defending its anemone or a clutch of eggs. Add a second pair only if the aquarium is more than 5 feet (1.5 m) long.
   Species requiring similar care: Ocellated Clownfish, *Amphiprion ocellaris,* 2–3 inches (5–8 cm). **Pink Skunk,** *Amphiprion perideraion* (see page 52), 2–3 inches (5–8 cm).

Yellow Tang
Zebrasoma flavescens (see photo, page 15)
   Family: Surgeonfish (Acanthuridae)
   Size: 2–6 inches (5–15 cm).
   Care: Needs fine sand, which it ingests to improve digestion of its food.
   Diet: Algae, small crustaceans (also frozen food).
   Compatibility: Very dominant fish, requiring ample room. Keep only one specimen, because territorial battles between Yellow Tangs can end in death.
   Species requiring similar care: Purple Tang, *Zebrasoma xanthurum* (see photo, right), 4–6 inches (10–15 cm). **Desjardin's Sailfin Tang,** *Zebrasoma desjardini* (see page 44), 4–6 inches (10–15 cm).

Young Purple Tang
(Zebrasoma xanthurum).

Palette Tang
Paracanthurus hepatus (see photo, page 15)
   Family: Surgeonfish (Acanthuridae)
   Size: 2–8 inches (5–20 cm).
   Care: Needs fine sand, which it ingests to improve digestion of its food. Somewhat susceptible to illness; therefore, acclimation period at pet store should last four to six weeks.
   Diet: Algae, small crustaceans (also frozen food). Also eats large quantities of higher algae.
   Compatibility: To avoid territorial battles, keep only one specimen per aquarium.
   Species requiring similar care: Yellow Eye Tang (Bristletooth Surgeonfish, Yellow-Eyed Surgeon), *Ctenochaetus strigosus* (see page 51), 3–4 inches (15–20 cm).

Green Chromis
Chromis viridis (see photo, page 12)
   Family: Damselfish (Pomacentridae)
   Size: 2–2.5 inches (5–7 cm).
   Care: Keep a school of at least four specimens.
   Diet: Small crustaceans (also frozen food).
   Compatibility: Eats very quickly; take care that slower-eating fish get their fair share at feeding time.
   Species requiring similar care: Blue Orangetail (Blue Damselfish, Blue Devil

Flame Angelfish.

Yellow Wrasse.

Damselfish), *Chrysiptera cyanea,* 2–2.5 inches (5–7 cm). **Azure Damselfish,** *Chrysiptera parasema* (see page 50), 2–2.5 inches (5–7 cm).

Longnosed Hawkfish
Oxycirrhites typus (see photo, pages 6–7)
    Family: Hawkfish (Cirrhitidae)
    Size: 2–4 inches (5–10 cm).
    Care: Can leap out of the water if alarmed; cover the aquarium.
    Diet: Small crustaceans (also frozen food).
    Compatibility: Do not keep with small shrimp; it will eat them.

Royal Gramma.

Species requiring similar care: Flame **Hawkfish,** *Neocirrhites armatus* (see page 48), 2–3 inches (5–8 cm). **Banded Hawkfish,** *Cirrhitichthys falco* (see page 64), 2–3 inches (5–8 cm).

Mandarin Fish.

Clown Anemonefish.

Yellow Tang.

Dragon Sleeper.

Mandarin Fish

Synchiropus splendidus (see photo, page 1)
Family: Dragonets (Callionymidae)
Size: 2–3 inches (5–8 cm).
Care: Demanding; not for beginners. Needs mini-reef environment where it can hunt for food among corals, algae, rocks; allow aquarium conditions to settle for at least three months before introducing this fish.

Diet: Algae, small crustaceans (also small frozen food, such as brine shrimp, mysids).
Compatibility: Never keep two males together (territorial battles will ensue). The first dorsal fin ray is longer in the male.
Special feature: A fish can leap out of the aquarium during courtship display; cover the aquarium.
Species requiring similar care: Spotted Mandarin, *Synchiropus picturatus* (see page 42), 1.5–2.5 inches (4–7 cm).

Yellow Wrasse

Halichoeres chrysus (see photo, page 14)
Family: Wrasses (Labridae)
Size: 2.5–3 inches (5–8 cm).

Palette Tang.

Care: Needs fine to medium substrate, about 1 inch (2 cm) deep, as it likes to bury itself in the sand at night. If two are kept, the larger will become male.

Diet: Small crustaceans (also frozen food).

Compatibility: Readily compatible with all fish species.

Species requiring similar care: Six-lined Wrasse (Pajama Wrasse), *Pseudocheilinus hexataenia* (see page 33), 2.5–3 inches (6–8 cm). **Cleaner Wrasse,** *Labroides dimidiatus* (see page 57), 2.5–3 inches (6–8 cm); grooms parasites from other fish and does not require sand substrate.

Bicolor Blenny

Ecsenius bicolor (see photo, page 59)
 Family: Blennies (Blenniidae)
 Size: 2–3 inches (5–8 cm).
 Care: Needs tunnels and holes in rocks for sleeping. Partly herbivorous; eats algae growing in the aquarium and will keep tank free of detrimental filamentous algae. Recommended for every aquarium.
 Diet: Algae, small crustaceans (also frozen food).
 Compatibility: Because normal algae growth will adequately feed only one fish, and because territorial battles are common, keep just one specimen.

Species requiring similar care: Banded Blenny (Sailfin/Algae Blenny), *Salarias fasciatus,* 3–5 inches (8–12 cm). **Black Benny,** *Altrosalarias fascus,* 3–5 inches (8–12 cm).

Dragon Sleeper

Amblygobius phalaena (see photo, page 15)
 Family: Gobies (Gobiidae)
 Size: 3–5 inches (8–12 cm).
 Care: Needs fine coral sand, which it takes into its mouth and sifts through the gills.
 Diet: Algae, small crustaceans (also frozen food). Keeps the aquarium free of bluish green algae.
 Compatibility: Compatible with all fish species. Purchase as a pair.
 Species requiring similar care: Bluebar-Cheek Gudgeon, *Eleotriodes strigatus* (see page 56), 3–5 inches (8–12 cm).

Flame Angelfish

Centropyge loriculus (see photo, page 14)
 Family: Angelfishes (Pomacanthidae)
 Size: 2–2.5 inches (5–7 cm).
 Care: As for surgeonfish (see page 13).
 Diet: Algae, small crustaceans (also frozen food).
 Compatibility: Do not keep with a similarly colored flame angelfish (territorial battles). If you want two specimens, it's best to purchase a pair.
 Special feature: May nip at coral polyps.
 Species requiring similar care: Flameback Angel, *Centropyge acan-*

*Hawkfish rest on rocks
and coral to survey
their surroundings.*

thops, 2–3 inches (5–8 cm). **Coral Beauty**, *Centropyge bispinosus*, 2–3 inches (5–8 cm).

Royal Gramma

Gramma loreto (see photo, page 14)
   Family: Fairy Basslets (Grammidae)
   Size: 2–3 inches (5–8 cm).
   Care: Needs rocks with small caves; very hardy.
   Diet: Small crustaceans (also frozen food).
   Compatibility: Because of territorial behavior, do not keep with similarly colored basslets.
   Special characteristics: Lines a cave with higher algae for spawning.
   Species requiring similar care: Blackcap Basslet, *Gramma melacara* (see page 38), 2–3 inches (5–8 cm). **Fridman's Dottyback (Black Basslet, Orchid Dottyback),** *Pseudochromis fridmani* (see page 35), 2–2.4 inches (5–6 cm). **Bicolor Dottyback (False Gramma, Paccagnella's Dottyback),** *Pseudochromis paccagnellae*, 2–2.4 inches (5–6 cm).

Marine Betta

Colloplesiops altivelis (see photo, page 56)
   Family: Plesiopidae
   Size: 4–6 inches (10–15 cm).
   Care: Very hardy; needs a rock pile with relatively large crannies or ledges.
   Diet: Small crustaceans (also frozen food).
   Compatibility: Do not keep with small shrimp; it will eat them.
   Species requiring similar care: *Colloplesiops argus*, 4–7 inches (10–18 cm).

Kuda (Yellow) Seahorse

Hippocampus kuda (see photo, page 57)
   Family: Seahorses (Syngnathidae)
   Size: 2–4 inches (5–10 cm).
   Care: Food must be placed directly in the seahorse's swimming territory.

TIP

Species Conservation

The Washington Convention on International Trade in Endangered Species (CITES) of Wild Fauna and Flora provides for the protection of flora and fauna whose worldwide survival is threatened. Depending on how much protection is needed, various species are listed in categories I or II. Species threatened with extinction are listed in Appendix I. These animals may not be sold or bought without special permission.

   Being placed on one of the CITES appendices means only that special permits are needed before the animals can be imported into the United States. Within the United States, the Endangered Species Act of 1973 prohibits interstate transport, trade, or barter in any protected species.

   The profiles in this book describe only species that can legally be kept in captivity, bred, and sold or bartered. The species sold in pet shops comply with the endangered species regulations and can be purchased legally.

   Diet: Small crustaceans.
   Compatibility: Seahorses should not be placed in a mixed–fish tank.
   Special characteristics: Changes color from a muddy yellow to brown (camouflage, courtship display). The female deposits eggs in the male's brood pouch, where they are fertilized and develop until they hatch.
   Species requiring similar care: All seahorses and pipefish.

Magnificent Ritteri Anemone.

Yellow Button Polyps.

Corals

On the following pages are profiles of several corals that combine well and are easy to care for, even for the novice aquarist. Stony corals are not included here, as they are quite difficult to maintain successfully.

Toadstool Coral, Gold Crown Coral
Sarcophyton glaucum
Family: Alcyoniidae
Size: 2–12 inches (5–30 cm).
Care: Needs a location with ample water movement and full-spectrum light. Susceptible to well-camouflaged nudibranchs (sea slugs) and parasitic crustaceans (see page 51).

Toadstool Coral (top), Soft Coral Tree (bottom).

Soft Coral Tree.

Diet: Primarily photosynthetic products of zooxanthellae; also dissolved organic substances, plankton.

Compatibility: Can be readily combined with nearly all other invertebrates and with all fish species.

Special characteristics: Regularly sloughs off its outer layer. The polyps are drawn in, and a thin transparent skin separates. Buds that break

Green Star Polyps.

Giant Button Polyps (Sea Mat).

Umbrella Xenia.

Cauliflower Coral

Cladiella sp. (see photo, page 18)

Family: Alcyoniidae

Size: 2–10 inches (5–25 cm).

Care: Needs a location with moderate water movement and full-spectrum light. Susceptible to well-camouflaged nudibranchs.

Diet: Primarily photosynthetic products of zooxanthellae; also dissolved organic substances, plankton.

Compatibility: Sensitive to adjacent stinging corals (such as sea anemones); keep a handbreadth between them.

off attach themselves to the bottom and form a new colony.

Species requiring similar care: *Sarcophyton ehrenbergi,* 2–12 inches (5–30 cm). **Finger Coral,** *Sinularia polydactyla,* 2–12 inches (5–30 cm), forms many shoots and can take up a good deal of room over time. **Cabbage Coral,** *Lobophytum crassum,* 2–16 inches (5–40 cm).

Disc Anemones (Mushroom Corals).

TIP

What Are Invertebrates?

Corals, crustaceans, starfish, sea urchins, snails, insects, arachnids, and many other lower animals are called invertebrates because they lack a backbone or spinal column. Corals are colonial marine polyps that rely for food primarily on symbiotic algae, known as zooxanthellae, that live within their tissue and supply the corals with oxygen and other nutrients produced by photosynthesis. Corals also open their mouths to ingest organic substances dissolved in the water, as well as plankton. Some sea anemones also eat small crustaceans and fish.

Special characteristics: Can grow very fast, increasing in size by up to 50 percent within one month.

Species requiring similar care: Soft Coral Tree, *Litophyton arboreum,* 2–16 inches (5–40 cm). **African Bush,** *Lemnalia africana,* (see page 21), 2–6 inches (5–15 cm).

Umbrella Xenia
Xenia umbellata (see photo, page 19)
   Family: Xenias (Xeniidae)
   Size: 2–3 inches (5–8 cm).
   Care: Requires moderate water circulation, especially abundant light, and an adequate iodine concentration; needs ample room, as it grows very fast.
   Diet: Primarily photosynthetic products of zooxanthellae; also dissolved organic substances, plankton.
   Compatibility: Best not to combine with *Litophyton arboreum,* stony corals, or Flame Angelfish.
   Special characteristics: Actively pulses its tentacles (waves them like grasping hands) to take in oxygen from the water flowing past.
   Species requiring similar care: *Xenia* sp. (variously called Thin Bar, Glove, Pom Pom, Silver Tip), 2–3 inches (5–8 cm), brownish. **Giant Anthelia,** *Anthelia glauca,* 2–3 inches (5–8 cm), does not pulse.

Disc Anemone, Mushroom Coral
Discosoma sp. (see photo, page 19)
   Family: Discosomatidae
   Size: 2–2.5 inches (5–7 cm).
   Care: Disc anemones are robust and adapt well to aquarium conditions. They occur in various colors and patterns. In general, deep blue and spotted disc anemones require less light than red and striped species. They do well under fluorescent light, manage with little water movement, and survive even if the water quality is poor.
   Diet: Primarily photosynthetic products of zooxanthellae; also plankton and small crustaceans.

Caution! Sea anemones sting; always wear gloves when handling these handsome creatures.

Compatibility: Like other anemones, disc anemones use stinging cells to repel their neighbors. For this reason, it's best to keep them a handbreadth away from nearby corals.

Special characteristics: Live in colonies and can proliferate rapidly by division. Disc anemones can ingest plankton and small crustaceans through their central mouth opening.

Species requiring similar care: Elephant Ear Coral, *Metarhodactis sp.,* 2–12 inches (5–30 cm). *Ricordea* sp., 2–3 inches (5–8 cm).

Giant Button Polyps, Sea Mat
Palythoa sp. (see photo, page 19)

Family: Zoanthidae

Size: Individual polyps about 1–2 inches (2–4 cm).

Care: Very easy to maintain in an aquarium. Needs abundant light. As in other photosynthetic organisms, if light is not sufficient, the zooxanthellae cannot provide sufficient nutrients, and the diet must be supplemented with small crustaceans.

Diet: Primarily photosynthetic products of zooxanthellae; also plankton and small crustaceans.

Compatibility: Attacks adjacent corals with stinging cells; therefore, always keep them a handbreadth away from the nearest corals.

Special characteristics: These anemones form colonies. With their small tentacles, they can grasp tiny prey as it swims past and convey the food to their mouth openings.

Species requiring similar care: Yellow Polyps, *Parazoanthus* sp. (see page 18), 0.5–1 inch (1–2 cm). **Button Polyps,** *Zoanthus* sp., 1–2 inches (2–5 cm).

Green Star Polyps
Clavularia viridis (see photo, page 19)

Family: Clavulariidae

Leather corals and soft corals, like the African Bush (Lemnalia africana), are hardy and generally problem-free aquarium dwellers.

Size: Polyps grow to about 0.4–0.6 inches (1–1.5 cm) and can spread over wide areas on a firm substrate.

Care: Requires a location with very abundant light and water movement.

Diet: Primarily photosynthetic products of zooxanthellae; plankton.

Compatibility: Sensitive to filamentous algae; their overgrowth deprives the coral of essential light.

Special characteristics: Forms tubes into which the polyp can withdraw if danger

threatens. Proliferates by sending out lateral shoots.

Species requiring similar care: Sea Stalk, *Briareum* sp., size as for *Clavularia viridis*.

Carpet Anemone

Stichodactyla haddoni (see illustration, page 28)

Family: Stichodactylidae

Size: 8–16 inches (20–40 cm) in diameter.

Care: Requires abundant light and only slight water movement. Can "migrate" about the aquarium; in general, it will find its own optimum location.

Caution: Carpet anemones have stinging cells that can cause skin irritation; keep hands away from their tentacles.

Giant Clam (Tridacna maxima) with starfish. Shell collectors have taken so many that giant clams are a protected species.

Diet: Photosynthetic products of zooxanthellae; crustaceans, mollusks, small fish, plankton.

Compatibility: Stings fiercely. All other corals should be kept at least 4 inches (10 cm) away. They can kill aquarum fish.

Special characteristics: The size of this anemone depends on its food supply. If kept along with anemonefish the diameter of the anemone should be at least three times the length of the largest anemonefish.

Species requiring similar care: Magnificent Ritteri Anemone, *Heteractis magnifica*.

Crustaceans, Starfish, and Other Invertebrates

Red Hermit Crab

Paguristes cadenati

Family: Diogenidae

Size: 1.5 inches (3 cm).

Care: Needs hiding places and stable salt concentrations. Because its abdomen (unlike that of other species) is not protected by a shell of chitin, the hermit crab occupies abandoned snail shells, moving from one to another as it grows. Provide an ample variety of appropriate sizes.

Diet: Filamentous algae growing in the aquarium; remnants of fish food.

Compatibility: Can readily be kept with several of the same species and with corals.

Special characteristics: Molts (sheds its shell); the shell quickly disintegrates in the aquarium.

Species requiring similar care: Hermit Crab, *Calcinus tubularis,* 1 inch (2 cm).

Cleaner Shrimp

Lysmata amboinensis (see photo, page 24)

Family: Hippolytidae

Size: 1.5–2.5 inches (3–6 cm).

Care: Needs hiding places and stable salt concentrations.

Diet: Remnants of fish food, plankton, fish parasites.

Compatibility: Can be kept with several shrimp of the same or different species.

Special characteristics: Removes parasites from the skin, gills, and mouth of fish. Cleaner shrimp are bisexual. They shed their shells, which disintegrate in the aquarium.

Species requiring similar care: Fire Shrimp, *Lysmata debelius* (see page 49), 1.5–2 inches (3–5 cm).

Hermit crabs move into a new snail shell when they outgrow the old one.

Banded Coral Shrimp

Stenopus hispidus (see photo, page 24)

Family: Stenopodidae

Size: 1.5–2.5 inches (3–6 cm).

Care: Needs hiding places and stable salt concentrations.

Diet: Remnants of fish food, plankton.

Compatibility: Unlike cleaner shrimp, these are not bisexual and should be kept in pairs if possible. If a mated pair cannot be obtained, keep only one specimen per aquarium. The female is wider than the male and has green on her back.

Species requiring similar care: *Stenopus grazilis,* 1–1.5 inches (2–3 cm).

India Starfish

Fromia indica (see illustration, page 28)

Family: Ophidiasteridae

Size: 2–3.5 inches (5–9 cm).

Care: Needs live rock supporting sponges and algae as source of food; for this reason, introduce only after aquarium has been established for at least three months.

Diet: Algae, sponges, organic detritus.

Compatibility: Needs sponges and algae to survive for long in an aquarium.

Species requiring similar care: Orange Starfish, *Fromia monilis,* 2.5–4 inches (6–10 cm); **Blue Linckia,** *Linckia laevigata,* 4–8 inches (10–20 cm).

Variegated Urchin

Lytechinus variegatus (see photo, page 25)

Family: Toxopneustidae

Cleaner Shrimp.

Banded Coral Shrimp.

Size: 2.5–3 inches (6–8 cm).

Care: Requires algae growing on rocks and stable salt concentrations. Use caution when placing in the aquarium; the sharp spines can cause painful punctures.

Diet: Algae, remnants of fish food, eels.

Compatibility: Sea urchins keep algae growth in check; don't keep too many, or they will eat the aquarium reef bare.

Species requiring similar care: Long-spined Sea Urchin, *Diadema setosum* (see page 25), 4–6 inches (10–15 cm).

Turban Snail.

Tapestry Turban Snail
Turbo petholatus

Family: Turbinidae

Size: 1.5–2.5 inches (3–6 cm).

Care: Requires algae growing on rocks.

Diet: Algae.

Compatibility: Readily compatible with all species. Excellent for limiting unwanted algae growth.

Hermit Crab.

Magnificent Feather Duster.

Variegated Urchin.

Long-spined Sea Urchin.

Species requiring similar care: *Tectus niloti-cus*, 1.5–3 inches (3–7 cm); **Fluctuating Turban,** *Turbo fluctuosus*, 1.5–2 inches (3–5 cm).

Magnificent Feather Duster
Sabellastarte magnifica
   Family: Tube Worms (Sabellidae)
   Size: 1.5–3 inches (3–8 cm).
   Care: Needs sandy substrate or rocks with holes. Suitable only for aquarium with ample plankton population.
   Diet: Feeds solely on plankton (including freeze-dried).
   Special characteristics: These worms construct leathery tubes that attach to the sand or rocks. When danger threatens, they contract their plankton-trapping tentacles into the tubes. When under stress—for example, when startled—they shed the tentacles, which will grow back.
   Species requiring similar care:
Fan Worm, *Spirographis spallanzanii*, 2–3 inches (5–8 cm).

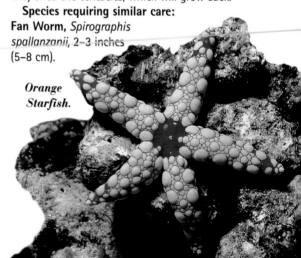

Orange Starfish.

TIP

Regulating Algae Growth

When the aquarium stock includes higher algae, the following problems may arise:

✔ The algae grow very rapidly and threaten the corals.

Remedy: Harvest excess algae by hand at regular intervals.

✔ The fish eat all the algae.

Remedy: Create a boundary (for example, with netting) to establish a fish-free zone where algae cannot be eaten. Take care, however, that the algae field receives adequate water circulation and light. You might also plant more *Halimeda* algae, because the browsing fish don't damage these as much as they do the *Caulerpa* species.

Clathrina clathrus (Sponge)

Clathrina clathrus

Family: Clathrinidae

Size: 3 inches (8 cm).

Care: Dark location with ample water movement.

Diet: Feeds solely on live plankton; will not eat freeze-dried plankton.

Compatibility: Do not keep in company with nudibranchs, which will eat it.

Species requiring similar care: *Acanthella carteri*, 4–12 inches (10–30 cm); *Callyspongia monilata*, 4–12 inches (10–30 cm).

Giant Clam

Tridacna maxima (see photo, page 22)

Protected Species: CITES Category II.

Family: Tridacnidae

Size: 2–12 inches (5–30 cm).

Care: Like corals, subsists on photosynthesis carried out by symbiotic algae (zooxanthellae) and hence requires ample light. Choose only locations where few people pass by, as the clam has sensitive reflex response to changes in light.

Diet: Photosynthetic products (zooxanthellae); plankton.

Compatibility: Do not keep with too many Flame Angelfish and Green Chromis, which pluck at the clam's edges. Shrimp, crabs, and certain mollusks may attack them.

Special characteristics: Forms protective substances against UV light. If aquarium lighting has a high UV content, the clam will gradually turn green or blue.

Higher Algae

Higher algae are an essential component of the marine aquarium ecosystem. They serve as decoration and, more important, as a source of nutrients; they also remove dissolved nitrogen compounds and phosphate from the water, thus improving its quality. In an aquarium with invertebrates, no single species of algae should cover more than 20 percent of the aquarium floor, because monocultures can deplete the water of essential trace elements. Filamentous algae and bluish green algae can be a problem; they proliferate at an alarming rate, especially with poor water quality or incorrect lighting (see page 48).

Caulerpa taxifolia

Caulerpa taxifolia

Family: Caulerpas (Caulerpaceae)

Size: In strong light, the algae field doubles within a week; it can completely take over an aquarium.

Care: Needs light; harvest regularly.

Compatibility: Surgeonfish can demolish a good stand of this algae within a short time;

screen off the algae (with netting or a separate tank).

Species requiring similar care: Other *Caulerpa* species (Grape Caulerpa, *C. racemosa; C. cupressoides*); red algae (*Halymenia* sp., *Chondria littoralis*).

Sea Cactus, Money Plant
Halimeda opuntia
　Family: Chlorophyta
　Size: Colony height is 4–8 inches (10–20 cm).
　Care: Needs light; harvest regularly; grows more slowly than *Caulerpa*.
　Compatibility: A good stand can be maintained even with herbivorous fish, because they are not devoured as eagerly as *Caulerpa*.

Grape Caulerpa (Caulerpa racemosa), left, and Sea Cactus (Halimeda opuntia), right.

　Species requiring similar care: Mermaid's Fan (*Udotea spinulosa*), 2–6 inches (5–15 cm).

Hydralithon boergeseni
Hydralithon boergeseni (see photo, page 59)
　Family: Rhodophyta
　Size: Can completely cover rocks and glass surfaces.
　Care: Considered an indicator of good water quality; if water quality is poor, filamentous algae will thrive. Use liquid calcium supplements.
　Compatibility: Use caution; a population of sea urchins will devour these red algae.

When planning your aquarium, you must be sure that the aquarium size, the equipment that controls water quality, and the plants and animals you choose are all suited to one another. On these pages are three sample aquarium plans. Refer to the table on page 37 for needed technology; see page 48 for feeding tips. You may substitute species requiring similar care (see species profiles on pages 12–27). Be sure to check daily that ammonia and nitrates are low.

Aquarium with Fish, Algae, and Invertebrates

Tank size: 80 gallons (300 L).

Water temperature: 75–80°F (24–27°C).

Water quality: Nitrate concentration below 30 ppm (mg/L); phosphate below 0.25 ppm (mg/L).

Stocking schedule: (After placing seawater)

✔ After 1 week: Live rock

✔ After 2 weeks: Algae (e.g., *Caulerpa*)

✔ After 3 weeks: Leather corals (e.g., *Sarcophyton*), disc anemones, and button polyps.

✔ After 4 weeks: 1 carpet anemone, 2–3 snails, 1 sea urchin, 5 Green Chromis, 1 Bicolor Blenny

✔ After 5 weeks: 1 pair Royal Gramma

✔ After 6 weeks: Soft corals, tube corals, 1 pair Clown Anemonefish, 1 Yellow Tang

✔ After 7 weeks: 1 sponge, 1 pair Dragon Sleepers

✔ After 3 months: 1 Giant Clam, starfish (2–3 *Fromia* or 1 *Linckia*), tube worms.

1 Yellow Tang, 2 Toadstool Coral, 3 Cauliflower Coral, 4 Giant Button Polyps, 5 Royal Gramma, 6 Disc Anemone, 7 Caulerpa, 8 Clown Anemonefish, 9 Carpet Anemone, 10 India Starfish, 11 Sea Urchin, 12 Dragon Sleeper, 13 Xenia coral, 14 Green Chromis, 15 live rock with algae, 16 Turban Snail.

AQUARIUM

General Rules

Never place animals and plants in fresh seawater. Wait to stock the aquarium until the water has stood long enough for the pH to stabilize, normally 4–5 days. When stocking the aquarium, follow the order described in the examples.

Rule of thumb for introducing corals: Always leave a handbreadth between one coral and the next. For each three feet (1 m) of aquarium length, there should be no more than ten corals, about 4–6 inches (10–15 cm) in size; otherwise, they will compete for space.

Rule of thumb for introducing fish: Begin with the more peaceable species. Introduce fish that prefer live food (such as Mandarins) last. Allow at least two gallons of water for each inch of fish (3 L for 1 cm).

Fish Aquarium with Algae

Tank size: 80 gallons (300 L).

Water temperature: 75–80°F (24–27°C).

Water quality: Nitrate concentration below 50 ppm (mg/L); phosphate about 0.25 ppm (mg/L).

Lighting: 4 fluorescent tubes.

Marine Betta.

Seahorse Aquarium

Tank size: 50 gallons (200 L).

Water temperature: 75–80°F (24–27°C).

Water quality: Nitrate concentration less than 30 ppm (mg/L); phosphate less than 0.25 ppm (mg/L).

Stocking schedule: After placing seawater in the aquarium, follow this order:
✔ After 1week: Live rock
✔ After 2 weeks: Algae (e.g., *Caulerpa*)
✔ After 3 weeks: Leather corals, disc anemones
✔ After 4 weeks: Snails, sea urchin, 1 Bicolor Blenny,

Palette Tang.

Stocking schedule: After placing seawater in the aquarium, follow this order:
✔ After 1week: Live rock, algae (e.g., *Caulerpa*)
✔ After 4 weeks: 1 pair Flame Angelfish, 1 Marine Betta
✔ After 6 weeks: 2 sea urchins, 5 Green Chromis, 1 pair Longnosed Hawkfish
✔ After 8 weeks: 1 Yellow Wrasse, 1 Palette Tang

1 pair seahorses
✔ After 6 weeks: Tube worms, 2 additional pairs of seahorses, 1 pair Mandarin Fish.

Seahorses change color.

AQUARIUM INSTALLATION AND EQUIPMENT

The well-being of your marine aquarium community depends on good water quality, a constant temperature and salt concentration of the water, and proper lighting in the aquarium. To guarantee these essential elements, you must install the necessary technical equipment.

What Does a Marine Aquarium Need?

In addition to the tank itself and the stand or cabinet that supports it, a functioning marine aquarium needs certain technical equipment (pumps and filters) to ensure water quality, a heating system, and lights. When purchasing these items, consider the aquarium as a total system. The aquarium's size and the equipment you install must be appropriate for the animals and plants you intend to maintain.

For a novice aquarium hobbyist, matching aquarium stock with the right equipment can be an overwhelming task. If you are planning your first marine aquarium, seek advice from a knowledgeable retailer. Look for equipment that has been designed as a complete system by a single manufacturer; this helps to ensure that the various components are optimally compatible. Purchase only high-quality equipment; this is not the place to economize.

For an idea of what you will need, refer to the table (*Technical Equipment*) on page 37. The table outlines systems to support the three

Invertebrates, such as shrimp and clams, place high demands on water quality.

sample aquarium plans recommended here (see pages 28–29).

The Aquarium

The size of the tank depends on the living creatures that will inhabit it. To create a viable biotope, however, your aquarium must meet certain minimum requirements:

✔ An aquarium with corals should have a capacity of at least 50 to 80 gallons (about 200–300 L).

✔ For a fish aquarium, the size and number of fish is the deciding factor. The minimum capacity is 25 gallons (about 100 L).

✔ A reef aquarium that combines fish, corals, and other invertebrates must have a capacity of 80 to 160 gallons (300–600 L) to accommodate the space requirements of many different species.

If the tank capacity is less than 50 gallons (200 L), the cost of equipment for an effective aquarium system is relatively high. As a result, systems designed for small tanks often include only the basics. This is not a good choice for a novice, however; such a system probably will not maintain adequate water quality on its own, and you will need to change the water very frequently (see page 46).

Safety and Legal Issues

Water damage and insurance: The water damage that could result from an overflowing or leaky aquarium can be quite costly. Therefore, before purchasing your aquarium, have it included in your homeowner's or renter's insurance and find out what the coverage includes.

Protection from electrical accidents: Because electricity and water is a dangerous combination, the electrical appliances needed for an aquarium are subject to special safety requirements. When buying electrical equipment, look for the UL mark that indicates the item complies with the safety standards established by the Underwriters Laboratories, Inc. and carefully follow the manufacturer's instructions. The use of an electronic circuit breaker that will interrupt the flow of electricity if there is damage to appliances or wiring is strongly recommended. Both pet stores and hardware stores also sell devices that sound an alarm if there is even a minor defect in wiring or appliances. Always unplug all electrical systems when working in the aquarium. Have repairs done only by a trained professional, and hire a licensed electrician if special wiring is needed.

Renter's rights: Even if your lease prohibits pets, an aquarium might be allowed. Ask when you rent, or ask before you invest in an aquarium. Your landlord may ask for a modest deposit to cover water damage.

Another important consideration for the marine aquarium is the proportions of the tank. A filled aquarium looks narrower than it really is. Therefore, it's advisable to choose minimum dimensions of 20 to 27 inches (50–70 cm) height and depth. Remember that deeper aquariums require more intense lighting than shallower ones.

Strength of the glass: The greater the volume of water in the aquarium, the stronger the glass walls should be. If the height is greater than 24 inches (60 cm), the glass should be 0.47 inch (12 mm) thick; if the height is greater than 27 inches (70 cm), it should be 0.6 inch (15 mm) thick.

Aquarium Placement

✔ A dark location is best. In a sunny window, seasonal variations in temperature and light are detrimental to water quality; the summer sun will be too hot, and the light promotes rampant algae growth.

✔ A grounded electric outlet must be nearby. In general, one or two wall outlets will not suffice; it will be necessary to add a multiple-outlet power strip.

✔ The floor must support the total weight of the aquarium. An 80-gallon (300-L) tank, complete with water, glass, stand, equipment, rocks, and sand, can weigh about 1100 pounds (500 kg). Before you set up your aquarium, check with your landlord or a builder to be sure the floor will support the load.

✔ The location must be level. If it is not, an aquarium held together with silicon adhesive might burst, causing extensive water damage. Be especially careful about floors with irregular spaces (containing insulation) below the surface. You can test the floor with a straightedge and a bubble level. If you find less than a ½ inch (1 mm) of curvature across about 1 yard (1 m) of floor, the location is suitable. Slight irregularities can be equalized with plastic shims.

Stand or Cabinet

It's best to use a stand or cabinet specifically designed to support an aquarium and all the necessary equipment. Pet stores sell a variety of such stands; if you'd prefer a custom-built cabinet, consult a carpenter. A stand or cabinet made with particleboard may cost less, but keep in mind that it will not be water-resistant.

✔ The surface of the stand should be slightly larger than the base of the aquarium, so that the aquarium glass is somewhat protected against bumps and blows.

✔ Place a styrofoam pad, about 1/8 to 1/2 inch (3–10 mm) thick, between the stand and the base of the aquarium to cushion the base against slight irregularities in the stand or the floor.

Heating

Tropical saltwater aquariums are maintained at temperatures of 75–80°F (24–27°C). It is extremely important to keep these constant, because the aquarium inhabitants are cold-blooded creatures; their body temperature is determined by the ambient temperature. Tropical coral reefs vary only slightly in temperature throughout the entire year; in the Maldives, for example, the annual variation is less than 2°F (1°C). Ordinarily, an aquarium is heated with a thermostatically controlled heating element calibrated in degrees Fahrenheit (or degrees Celsius) and accurate to the nearest degree. In addition, the water temperature can be monitored with an aquarium thermometer. Aquarium heaters with digital thermostats, offering more precise regulation, are also available.

If the water temperature rises to above 85°F (30°C) because of hot summer weather, it will be necessary to cool the aquarium. First, remove the aquarium cover; this will lower the temperature by about 1°F (about 0.5°C). If you direct a fan at the water surface, the temperature will drop by an additional 2–4°F (1–2°C).

If the overheating is caused by appliances, such as pumps, a fluid chiller designed for aquariums may need to be purchased.

Special cooling equipment is required for Mediterranean aquariums and lobster tanks, which are maintained at lower temperatures.

Lighting

Proper lighting is important not only for the visual attractiveness of the aquarium, but especially for coral growth. The algae within the coral tissue require abundant light for photosynthesis, which yields oxygen and nutrients the corals need in order to thrive. Therefore, an aquarium containing corals should be equipped with lamps that offer strong illumination (50,000 to 100,000 lux), depending on its depth.

The Six-lined Wrasse browses over live rock in search of tiny crustaceans and mollusks to eat.

Also important is the wavelength of the light. Natural light includes a broad spectrum of wavelengths (from ultraviolet through blue, green, yellow, red, to infrared), which differ in how well they penetrate seawater. Most of the red light fraction is filtered out by the water, while the blue light penetrates deep into the ocean. To simulate the natural light that reaches a depth of about 16 to 50 feet (5–15 m), therefore, lamps with a higher proportion of blue light are used.

Almost all marine aquarium lighting systems use metal halide (HQI) lamps or fluorescent lamps.

Metal halide (HQI) lamps produce high-intensity light that is suitable for corals and

Showy and not at all shy, a damselfish is always an eye-catcher.

fish. They are so-called spot lamps and create a play of light and shadow in the aquarium, as the sun does in the ocean depths. This, in combination with the refraction of light on the water surface, gives metal halide lighting a very natural look. Metal halide lamps are generally more expensive than fluorescent lamps. Most metal halide aquarium lights are designed to hang above the tank.

Fluorescent lamps generally produce light of less intensity than metal halide lamps. Nevertheless, they are quite widely used, because they are available in a great variety of types that can be combined to create almost every conceivable mixture of light. Usually, daylight fluorescent bulbs are combined with actinic lamps (with a greater blue light fraction).

As a rule, fluorescent bulbs should be used with reflectors, which considerably increase the light intensity. If fluorescent light fixtures are attached to the edge of the aquarium, they must be waterproof. They should be made of corrosion-resistant anodized aluminum or plastic and comply with UL standards.

Photoperiod: With HQI lamps, the period of illumination should be about nine hours a day. When fluorescent lights are used, the aquarium should receive eleven to twelve hours of light each day. In a newly established aquarium, these times should be reduced by one or two hours for the first months, so as not to promote the growth of filamentous and blue-green algae. Many light fixtures are designed to provide the proper amount of light for marine invertebrates and plant aquariums.

Water Circulation

Specially designed pumps can create a flow of water within the aquarium. This distributes warmth, oxygenated water, and plankton around the tank and transports waste products and other harmful substances dissolved in the water to the filter for removal.

Points to remember:

✔ The water must be able to flow around the tank without being blocked by rock structures (for example, see illustrations, page 41).

✔ The pump should circulate the tank contents five to ten times per hour and should have the largest possible outlet diameter, creat-

ing a gentle flow rather than a strong current. The lines of flow should be parallel and broad.

✔ During the period of darkness in the aquarium, reduce the water flow; in a natural coral reef, the current often diminishes during the night.

✔ Turn off the circulating and filter pumps during feeding; otherwise, the food will be removed as well. Some pumps have an automatic pause device for feeding time.

Modern circulating pumps are capable of imitating the natural dashing of waves, creating turbulence in the water that prevents the formation of deposits on the bottom and sides of the tank. With two circulating pumps and a timer to alternate between them, you can even simulate the natural ebb and flow of the tides.

Water Treatment

The oceans contain an enormous volume of water that brings about a natural cleaning process. In the aquarium, food remnants and the waste products of the marine organisms accumulate and produce harmful substances. Clean water must be restored with filters and pumps or by changing the water.

If you outfit your aquarium with good equipment for water treatment, you can maintain good water quality with only regular, small water changes. The necessary equipment includes filters, protein skimmers, and a means of controlling the specific gravity and salinity of the water.

Dottybacks like the Fridman's (Orchid) Dottyback are closely related to the Fairy Basslets.

Filters

Marine aquarists rely on various types of filters to purify the aquarium water. In *mechanical filters,* the aquarium water flows through pads, foam, sand, and other filter media. These remove particulate wastes, such as excrement and food and plant residues, before they decay and dissolve in the water. Certain bacteria in the water, using a high amount of oxygen, transform these organic products into various toxic substances, including ammonia. The aquarium's inhabitants can tolerate only very small amounts of these substances. To prevent the organic wastes from decaying in the filter, it must be cleaned regularly. The pad or other filter medium must be replaced once or twice a week. In the marine aquarium, it is particularly important for the surface water to be transported to the filter as well; otherwise, organic compounds will accumulate on the surface of the water, forming an unsightly scum. For this reason, the filtering apparatus should be equipped with a means of suctioning off the surface water.

Trickle filters (also called wet/dry filters) purify the water with the help of bacteria and fungi that proliferate in the filter substrate. These microorganisms feed on the toxic nitrogen compounds that form as organic wastes decay, converting them to less toxic substances. In the first step of this process, called nitrification, ammonia (NH_3) or ammonium (NH_4^+) is converted to nitrite (NO_2^-), and nitrite to nitrate (NO_3^-). This is an aerobic process, because the nitrifying bacteria use oxygen. Nitrate is moderately toxic to delicate fish and invertebrates and must be removed. Other bacteria, which are anaerobic, convert it to free nitrogen and oxygen. Trickle filters require a few weeks to reach their full efficacy, because the bacteria cultures take time to proliferate.

Absorption via activated carbon: The filter system must also include activated carbon (most filters have special compartments for this), which traps organic materials and particulate matter, leaving the water clear. Without this filter component, nitrogen-containing animal wastes and compounds from decomposing plant cells give the water an undesirable yellow cast.

The absorption capacity of activated carbon is very high initially, but it declines over time as the filter works. It is advisable to replace the carbon every 10 to 14 days.

Protein Skimmers

Protein skimmers, which remove dissolved organic materials—primarily protein from animal waste and food residues—from the water, are an essential piece of equipment for the saltwater aquarium. These devices produce small air bubbles that come in contact with the organic materials, forming a foam. Rising to the water surface, this foam is

Anemonefish are not sensitive to the stinging cells of their host anemone.

Technical Equipment in a Typical Aquarium (see pages 28–29)

	Aquarium with Fish, Algae, Invertebrates	Aquarium with Fish and Algae	Seahorse Aquarium
Aquarium Dimensions	*Size:* (L × W × H): 40 × 24 × 24 inches (100 × 60 × 60 cm) *Total capacity:* 95 gallons (360 L) *Filled volume:* about 80 gallons (about 300 L)	*Size:* (L × W × H): 40 × 24 × 24 inches (100 × 60 × 60 cm) *Total capacity:* 95 gallons (360 L) *Filled volume:* about 80 gallons (about 300 L)	*Size:* (L × W × H): 40 × 20 × 20 inches (100 × 50 × 50 cm) *Total capacity:* 66 gallons (250 L) *Filled volume:* about 53 gallons (about 200 L)
Standard Aquarium Equipment (installed in aquarium)	Flow pump (800 gallons/hr, 3000 L/hr); mechanical filter, trickle filter, protein skimmer, specific gravity/salinity tester, activated carbon filter medium, rod heater with thermostat, 1 HQI pendant lamp (150 or 200 watts)	Flow pump (800 gallons/hr, 3000 L/hr); mechanical filter, trickle filter, protein skimmer, specific gravity/salinity tester, activated carbon filter medium, rod heater with thermostat, 3–4 fluorescent lamps	Flow pump (400 gallons/hr, 1500 L/hr) with large outlet diameter (about 1 inch, about 2 cm); mechanical filter, trickle filter, protein skimmer, specific gravity/salinity tester, activated carbon filter medium, rod heater with thermostat, 1 HQI pendant lamp (150 watts) or 4 fluorescent lamps
Optional Equipment	Wave simulator, calcium reactor, electronic thermostat	Wave simulator, electronic thermostat	Wave simulator, calcium reactor, electronic thermostat
Equipment in Cabinet or Stand	Intake and return tubes, recirculating pump, flow pump in aquarium, glass container with cover	Intake and return tubes, recirculating pump, flow pump in aquarium, glass container with cover	Intake and return tubes, recirculating pump, flow pump in aquarium, glass container with cover
Standard Accessories	Hydrometer or conductivity meter, thermometer, pH test kit, a supply of filter media and activated carbon, water quality test kits	Hydrometer or conductivity meter, thermometer, pH test kit, a supply of filter media and activated carbon, water quality test kits	Hydrometer or conductivity meter, thermometer, pH test kit, a supply of filter media and activated carbon, water quality test kits

collected in a chamber that must be emptied and cleaned once a week. Some protein skimmers produce air bubbles from an air pump through diffusers (air stones), others with a pressure pump that pulls in atmospheric air. Devices with diffusers require regular replacement of the air stones to maintain full efficacy. Devices with pressure pumps or jets need less maintenance. If you use a protein skimmer with a pressure pump, be careful that the device does not harm the plankton in your aquarium by pulling them into the pump, where they are destroyed.

Salinity Regulation

Saltwater creatures are sensitive to variations in the salt concentration. In an aquarium, the salinity of the water increases as water evaporates. In oceans, the water lost to evaporation is replaced by rainfall or an influx of fresh water, and the salt balance remains stable. In the marine aquarium, the water must be replaced by other means. There are devices that automatically replenish the aquarium water as needed, pumping fresh water from a reservoir.

Note: In many areas of the United States, untreated water should not be added to aquariums. If your aquarium contains substances, such as metallic salts, phosphates, and nitrate, that accumulate over

time and contribute to excessive algae growth or even are toxic to aquatic life, use water treated by reverse osmosis, which filters salts and harmful substances out of tap water. (Pet stores sell this equipment.)

Calcium Reactor

Corals and algae, as they grow, deplete the calcium dissolved in the aquarium water. One way to replenish this nutrient is with a calcium reactor, which is filled with a pure form of calcium (calcium carbonate). Calcium reactors are generally used only in aquariums containing stony corals. It has been found, however, that such devices promote the growth of all other corals as well.

Housing the Aquarium Equipment

The equipment needed to maintain water quality is typically hidden out of sight in the aquarium cabinet, along with the additional tubes and pumps that are needed to carry the water from the aquarium to the equipment and back again.

Conditioning Your New Aquarium

Once you have set up your aquarium and installed the proper equipment, you can start the conditioning process by placing seawater in the tank. You can mix the seawater yourself.

Blackcap Basslet
(Gramma melacara).

Startup of a Fish and Invertebrate Reef-type Aquarium with Synthetic Seawater

✔ Sea salt mixes for marine aquariums are sold in pet stores. Following the manufacturer's instructions, place the correct amount of salt in the aquarium and fill the tank with water from a reverse-osmosis unit (see page 38).

✔ Turn on the filters, circulation pumps, and automatic water feed (if any). Protein skimmers and lights are not yet used.

✔ After a day or two, measure the salinity and make any necessary adjustments (see page 44).

✔ Let the water stand for at least 7–10 days. Sea salts combine with organic compounds and other substances to develop colloids, which protect animals and plants against disease. It takes several weeks for adequate colloid development to take place in the aquarium. If you introduce living organisms too soon, they will probably die.

✔ The next step is to add rocks inhabited by algae and microorganisms, which are known as "live rock" and are sold in pet stores. In an 80-gallon (300-L) aquarium, you should use about 65–110 pounds (30–50 kg) of this rock to build a reef. In the substructure of the reef, where light does not penetrate, you can also use 10–20 pounds (about 5–10 kg) of tuff (lava rock—see *Rock Reef*, page 40). The live rock gives the aquarium ecosystem greater stability in the startup phase. If you use only ordinary rock, algae monocultures will develop in the first few months; these inhibit the growth of coral and are unattractive as well. If you decide not to use live rock, you should at least start with a few tufts of Grape Caulerpa (*Caulerpa racemosa*) or Sea Cactus (*Halimeda opuntia*). Please note that if a fish-only aquarium is being set up, live rock is often not used.

✔ Spread coral sand as a substrate (see page 40).

✔ Turn on all the equipment used to control water quality. Turn on the aquarium lighting, but until you introduce the first invertebrates, the lights should be on for only six hours a day.

✔ Test all water quality parameters (see page 43). You must not introduce fish and invertebrates until these parameters are within the recommended range. Stock the aquarium gradually and in the appropriate order (see *HOW-TO: Stock the Aquarium*, pages 28–29).

Proper Water Flow

The basic requirement for proper water circulation in the aquarium is that the flow must be circular (see illustration). If the water flow is not blocked, for example by a reef of rocks, even relatively heavy particles of debris will be transported to the filter. You can still screen the equipment with rocks, but you must be sure that the pump outlets and the water intake areas are not blocked. Also take care that higher algae can't grow in front of the water intake area.

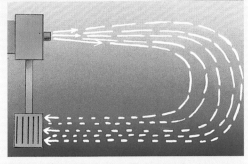

Flow pumps must be installed properly to create a circular flow

Introducing Aquarium Stock

Live rock: Keep the live rock wet with seawater as you transport it. If it dries out, the living creatures it shelters will die. At home, simply place the live rock in the aquarium.

Higher algae: For algae that will grow on the aquarium floor, bore a hole in the sand with your finger and place the algae in the hollow. If the algae are to grow on rocks, secure each tuft gently between two rocks or weight it down with small stones.

Corals: Most species grow attached to a rock. During transport, be careful that the coral polyps aren't squashed in the plastic bag.

Rock Reef and Substrate

✔ The rocks should rest on the glass floor without wobbling. To secure them, purchase from the pet store a special adhesive that is resistant to seawater. Use this to build a solid substructure of algae-free tuff, or lava rock. Then layer live rock on top of the substructure.

✔ If the rocks have sharp edges, protect the glass aquarium floor by setting them on a flat piece of rock or a piece of hard PVC plastic or acrylic.

✔ For constructing the reef, it's better to use large rocks and flat rocks rather than fist-sized or rounded rocks. It's also easier to establish corals on horizontal surfaces.

✔ Form little caves and ledges as you build. Reef dwellers need hiding places to feel safe and comfortable.

✔ Be careful not to block the outlets of circulating pumps and filter pumps with rocks.

✔ Apply the substrate (coral sand) after the reef is built. If you build the reef on sand, creatures that live in sand can tunnel under the reef and cause it to topple. The substrate should be about one inch (3 cm) deep.

AQUARIUM

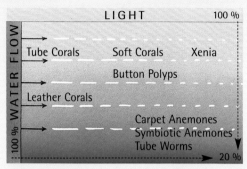

Corals and tube worms have very specific requirements in regard to light conditions and water flow.

Because corals are sensitive to variations in temperature and salinity, they must become acclimated to the temperature and salt concentration in your aquarium. Follow these steps as you gradually adjust the water in the bag to the conditions in the aquarium:

✔ Place the coral, in its bag, in a clean pail containing absolutely no detergent residues.

✔ With a cup, slowly add water from the aquarium to the bag, measuring the temperature and salinity of the water in the bag as you do so (see page 44).

✔ When the temperature and salinity are the same as in the aquarium (the salt concentration must not deviate by more than 3 mS/cm conductivity), it's safe to place the coral in the aquarium. It may be exposed to air for a brief time (a few seconds) during the transfer.

✔ The water can be returned to the aquarium along with the coral.

✔ Wear protective gloves when handling anemones, as they can sting. After a short time, they will attach themselves firmly to the solid substrate, rocks, or even glass. A small hollow made of stones can be helpful. Observe them for the first few days, because they might seek another spot. Do not let them settle in the intake area of filter or water flow pumps, or where they would sting other corals or block their light.

Fish: Introduce fish in the same way as corals, but keep the following points in mind:

Stones support the anemone as it attaches itself.

✔ The pail must be covered so that the fish can't jump out.

✔ When the temperature and salinity are adjusted, use a small net to transfer the fish into the aquarium.

✔ If a particular fish seems not to have adjusted to the new water conditions (for example, if it is not as active as it should be), you should not put it in the aquarium yet.

✔ Don't return the water in the pail to the aquarium, because it might be soiled with feces.

Sea urchins, starfish, crustaceans, and other invertebrates are transferred in the same way as fish.

Sponges must be kept under water at all times during the transfer.

Fish and invertebrates need gradual acclimation before they are put in the aquarium.

ROUTINE MAINTENANCE OF THE MARINE AQUARIUM

Your saltwater aquarium needs regular maintenance if its inhabitants are to grow and thrive. The routine procedures of aquarium care include tests to monitor the water quality, maintenance and cleaning of aquarium equipment, and feeding the fish and invertebrates in your marine community.

Monitoring Water Quality

The water quality in a marine aquarium is critically important for the health of animals and plants. The presence of harmful substances in the water will inevitably lead to disease (see page 50). You can test most water parameters quickly and reliably with the chemical test kits that are sold in pet stores. These kits contain chemicals in liquid and powder form. When mixed in a test tube with a sample of your aquarium water, the chemicals change color to indicate the concentration of dissolved substances. You should check the concentration of the following substances once a week:

Nitrogen compounds, which are highly toxic to fish, form when the water contains dissolved food residues, dead tissue, and animal wastes. Elevated concentrations may occur particularly during the startup phase of the aquarium and in a tank containing many fish. The causes include failure to clean the mechanical filter as often as needed or the use of inadequate protein skimmers or trickle filters (see pages 36 and 38).

Brilliant color in the aquarium: A damselfish (above) and a Spotted Mandarin.

You should monitor the following nitrogen compounds at regular intervals:

✔ Ammonia (NH_3^+) and ammonium (NH_4^+) occur together. Ideal concentrations are below 0.05 ppm (mg/L). High concentrations (0.1 to 0.2 ppm (mg/L)) must be avoided. Because these limits are below the detection level of many commercial tests, the fish may already be sick by the time ammonia and ammonium are detectable in the water.

✔ Nitrite (NO_2^-) forms when ammonia and ammonium are broken down by bacteria. Levels of 0.02 to 0.05 ppm (mg/L) are still tolerable. At levels of 0.1 ppm (mg/L) and higher, sensitive invertebrates and fish can suffer.

✔ Nitrate (NO_3^-) is a toxic nitrogen compound formed by the further degradation of nitrite. The acceptable limits are a matter of dispute. Concentrations below 20 ppm (mg/L) are generally considered desirable as a goal. Values of 50 to 80 ppm (mg/L) are tolerable. Levels above 120 ppm (mg/L) should definitely be avoided.

Phosphate (PO_4^{3+}), like nitrogen compounds, is dissolved in the water as a result of decomposition of organic wastes. If the phosphate concentration is too high, undesirable filamentous algae will grow rampant, quickly overgrowing the corals. Causes of excessive phosphate levels include overfeeding the fish or keeping too many fish in a tank whose water control system is inadequate to keep the water clean.

The phosphate concentration should be less than 0.2 ppm (mg/L) (the detection threshold of most quick tests). At levels between 0.2 and 0.7 ppm (mg/L), aquariums with invertebrates are considered moderately to severely stressed. In fish aquariums, the tolerance levels can be higher.

The carbonate hardness (KH) is a measure of the amount of calcium carbonate and magnesium carbonate dissolved in the water. These act as a buffer system in the seawater; that is, they neutralize acids and thereby limit changes in the pH value (see page 45) of the water. Ocean water naturally maintains a carbonate hardness of 6–9°dKH. In the marine aquarium, the carbonate hardness should be at least 7°dKH. Levels above 10°dKH are unnatural and should be avoided. To increase the carbonate hardness, calcium carbonate can be added to the water via a calcium reactor (see page 38) or in limewater (sold in pet stores).

Calcium (Ca_2^+) is an essential element for many invertebrates and must be added to the water regularly (use calcium reactor or limewater). Natural seawater contains about 410 ppm (mg/L) of dissolved calcium. If the concentration in the marine aquarium is lower than this, coral growth will be inhibited.

Copper (Cu_2^+) is present in seawater only in trace amounts. Copper should not be detectable in aquarium water. Medications that contain copper and are used to treat diseases in fish must never be used in an aquarium containing higher algae or corals (see page 50). Some tap water contains copper. Use a reverse osmosis apparatus to purify the water (see page 38).

Measuring Salinity

The salt concentration of the aquarium water should remain constant. However, evaporation or temperature changes may cause it to vary. The salt concentration is determined by measuring the conductivity or the density of the saltwater.

✔ The electrical conductivity can be measured within a few seconds using an electrode. Because conductivity varies with the water temperature, you should use only an apparatus with automatic temperature compensation.

✔ The density, or specific gravity, is measured with a hydrometer. This glass instrument is placed in the aquarium where it floats freely, sinking to a depth determined by the salt concentration and the temperature. At a water temperature of 77°F (25°C), the density should be between 1.022 and 1.024 g/cm.

Measuring specific gravity takes longer than measuring conductivity; also, temperature compensation is not automatic, so the method is less accurate.

The markings of Desjardin's Sailfin Tang are more distinct in older specimens.

Recommended Maintenance Schedule

Daily	Check aquarium equipment (heating, flow pumps, lighting, protein skimmers); check condition of fish and corals; feed.
Weekly	Clean mechanical filter (replace filter medium); empty and rinse collection chamber of protein skimmer; measure water parameters; clean glass.
Monthly	Change diffusers of air-pump-driven protein skimmers; inspect water lines for trickle filters.
Every three months	Inspect all aquarium equipment; clean nozzles of jet-driven protein skimmers; calibrate measurement equipment.
Once a year	Replace light bulbs (HQI bulbs; fluorescent bulbs need to be replaced more often).
As required	Harvest excess algae; if corals aren't growing well, move them to a more suitable site.

Measuring the Temperature

The temperature in the aquarium should be constant; the acceptable range is 77 to 80°F (25–27°C). Variations in temperature also mean variations in salinity, and they cause stress to the aquarium inhabitants (see *Heating*, page 33).

Measuring the pH

The pH value of a solution is a measure of its acidity or alkalinity. At a pH of 7.0, the solution is said to be neutral; below 7.0 it is acid, and above 7.0 it is alkaline. In the marine aquarium, the pH value should be between 8.1 and 8.4. It's best to measure the pH value with an electrical apparatus, because many of the chemical kits sold in stores are not sufficiently accurate for the marine aquarium.

The pH value varies throughout the day. During the hours of light, the value rises, because the photosynthetic activity of the algae removes carbonic acid (in the form of dissolved carbon dioxide, which the algae convert to oxygen) from the water. At night, as the algae respire, they give off carbon dioxide and the pH value decreases.

The pH value can sink to harmful levels when acids accumulate in the water as a result of the degradation of organic wastes. One way to prevent this is to add calcium carbonate (see *Carbonate Hardness*, page 44).

Measuring the Redox Potential

The redox potential is a measure of the organic substances present in the water and the availability of oxygen. The higher the redox potential, the lower the content of organic substances and the higher the oxygen content of the water. If an animal dies unnoticed, the redox potential in the aquarium drops rapidly.

The redox potential is measured with an electrical device. Because the redox potential is dependent on the temperature and pH of the water, these values must be taken into account, along with the type of electrode used. At 79°F

Solving Problems

Sign	Cause	Remedy
Water is cloudy (green or milky)	Algae bloom of suspended algae, death of a large mass of algae, dead animals. It may also be that corals, starfish, or mollusks have laid eggs in the water.	In case of algae bloom, turn skimmer to high. This phenomenon often occurs during the startup phase of an aquarium, but it soon clears up. If clouded water is caused by dead animals and algae, remove them.
Protein skimmer doesn't capture any foam.	No fish, or few fish, in the aquarium; fat content of food is too high.	If there are no fish in the aquarium yet, you can turn off the protein skimmer. Avoid fatty foods, which reduce the efficacy of the protein skimmer.
Bubbles in aquarium water.	High level of oxygen production by algae; bubbles sucked into water pump through leaky connections.	Action is needed only if bubble formation is extreme. Reduce lighting period, reduce nitrate and phosphate content, reduce amount of algae.
Fish swim lopsided.	Fish diseased or poisoned, for example, by injured poisonous sea cucumber.	Test for nitrite, ammonium; use activated carbon. Remove sea cucumber. Treat fish (see page 50).

(26°C) and pH 8.2, with a platinum electrode (the most common type of electrode), the redox potential should be about 300 millivolts. To reduce the risk of diseased fish, the redox potential can be increased artificially by introducing ozone to the water (pet stores sell the necessary equipment).

Note: Ozone is toxic. Use only as directed, taking all safety precautions.

Changing the Water

Whether and how often to change the water in a saltwater aquarium is a matter of dispute. At one time, changing the water was the only way to maintain water quality. Nowadays, however, with the right aquarium equipment and good routine maintenance, it is hardly ever nec-essary to change the water. Because the aquarium inhabitants experience stress each time the water is changed, the aquarium hobbyist should strive to maintain good water quality without changing the water.

When must a lot of water be changed? You should change the water whenever the level of ammonia, nitrite, nitrate, phosphate, or other such substances exceeds the specified limit, or whenever so-called bioindicators, such as rampant algae growth, suggest that conditions are not right. If the water is under continuous stress, for example, because the aquarium is overcrowded, you will generally need to change it every two to four weeks. A better solution, however, is to upgrade the aquarium equipment.

What is the right way to change the water?
✔ Procure seawater (see page 39) and let it stand for at least 24 hours (preferably 1 to 2 weeks). Use an air stone and flow pump to aerate and mix the water.
✔ Turn off all the aquarium equipment except the lights.
✔ Have a bucket ready with a capacity of at least 2½ gallons (10 L) and a piece of tubing 6–10 feet (2–3 m) long and at least ½ inch (12 mm) in diameter. Pinching both ends of the tube, place one end in the aquarium water and the other in the bucket on the floor beside the aquarium. Release the ends of the tube. The water will siphon through the tube and into the bucket.

How much water should be replaced?
✔ Replacing 10 percent of the water volume will mean no significant risk to plants and animals.
✔ Replacing 20–30 percent of the water volume may cause irritation to corals and fish.
✔ Changing more than 30 percent of the water disrupts the biological equilibrium of the aquarium, quite possibly with loss of animal life.

Dealing with Algae Problems

The accumulation of nitrogen compounds and phosphate, incorrect lighting, and a lack of herbivorous fish and invertebrates can lead to problematic growth of filamentous and blue-green algae in the aquarium. If this happens, the first step is to test the water for excess levels of nitrate and phosphate. If the concentrations are within the normal range, the most common cause of rampant algae growth is an incompatible selection of aquarium stock. Try adding more herbivorous fish and invertebrates.

Algae problems may also arise if large areas of the aquarium are left free for algae growth. Remove the excess algae and substitute live rock or corals.

VACATION CARE

If you don't have a reliable person to take care of your aquarium while you are away, you should make a few preparations:
✔ *When you first set up your aquarium, be sure to include a device to replenish the aquarium water from an ample reservoir; also, install an automatic feed dispenser for dry foods.*
✔ *Don't introduce new aquarium stock during the two or three weeks before you leave.*
✔ *Clean the filters and protein skimmer.*
✔ *Change the aquarium to "vacation mode" three to five days before your departure; this will give you time to make any necessary adjustments.*
✔ *Even with excellent automatic equipment to control water quality, you should not leave the aquarium unattended for more than two to three weeks.*
✔ *If you do have someone tending to your aquarium, be sure to explain the procedures for feeding and anything else that must be done while you are away. Leave the telephone number of the pet store for emergencies.*

When algae growth gets out of hand:
✔ Reduce the number of fish, if possible.
✔ Give less food.
✔ Maintain filters and protein skimmers at more regular intervals and increase their performance level.
✔ Reduce the period of lighting (5 to 6 hours). Check the strength of installed lighting; replace old HQI lamps as required. But be careful not to harm photosynthetic invertebrates.
✔ In the short term, it can be helpful to remove the algae by hand or with a suction tube and bucket. If you also replace 10 to 15 percent of the water each week, the nitrate and phosphate levels can decrease by half within a month or two. Without improving regular maintenance or upgrading the aquarium equipment, a long-term solution to algae problems will be almost impossible.

Feeding

Pet stores sell live, frozen, and dried food for your aquarium inhabitants. A combination of live and frozen food is recommended. Fish accept frozen food more readily than dried food, and the residues of frozen food are more easily removed by the equipment that cleans the water. You can resort to dry food with an automatic feed dispenser on a temporary basis when you are away from home, but fish must first be conditioned to accept it.

Fish, crustaceans, and other invertebrates: The most important food is small crustaceans such as brine shrimp *(Artemia)*, krill *(Euphausia superba)*, and mysids, as well as mosquito larvae. The size of the food should correspond to the size of the mouth opening (0.08 to 0.5 inch, 2–10 mm). The amount of food varies with the size of the animal.

Corals: Food for corals depends on the species and the amount of light they receive. Almost all corals subsist primarily on the products of photosynthesis carried out by their symbiotic zooxanthellae. The ideal supplement is living or frozen animal microplankton (size: less than 0.04 inch, 1 mm), such as brine shrimp, which are simply added to the water. This should be done regularly, for example, once a week. Some anemones also eat small crustaceans such as mysids, krill, and *Artemia*, which are given every one or two weeks with a feeding syringe or feeding tube (sold in pet stores). Symbiotic anemones also eat shrimp and bits of mollusks (size of morsels, about ½ to 1 inch, 1–3 cm).

Guidelines for Typical Aquariums

Aquarium with fish, algae, and invertebrates: Five times a week, 1 to 2 teaspoons of frozen *Artemia* or mysids. Once a week, animal microplankton and, for each carpet anemone, 2 morsels of shrimp.

Aquarium with fish and algae: Five times a week, 1 to 2 teaspoons of krill, mysids, and *Artemia*.

Seahorse aquarium: Five times a week, 1 teaspoon of live *Artemia* or mysids. Use a feeding syringe to place the food for seahorses within their swimming area.

The Flame Hawkfish feeds on small crustaceans.

7 Golden Rules
for Feeding

1 Always feed at the same time of day. Your fish will adjust to this routine.

2 The filter pumps must be turned off during feeding. Otherwise, food is drawn into the filter. There are devices that will automatically pause the filter and flow pumps for about ten minutes during feeding time.

3 Never give food that is still frozen; it must be thawed first. To thaw, place the frozen food in a glass of warm aquarium water.

4 The food must be the right size and shape for the animal's mouth.

5 Put the food in the tank a little at a time, so that there will not be uneaten leftovers on the bottom of the aquarium.

6 Some fish feed slowly and cautiously, while others are quick, voracious, and aggressive at feeding time. To ensure that all the fish have access to food, place it at several locations in the aquarium at the same time.

7 Provide suitable food for each species in your aquarium. Herbivores should have plant materials (algae) to eat, while carnivores need animal protein.

Preventive Care and Health Problems

The most important element for a healthy aquarium community is good water quality. In a well-tended aquarium, diseases are rare. These factors may cause health problems:

✔ Introduction of new or diseased animals, and not quarantining new fish for 3 weeks.

✔ High nitrite or ammonia concentrations.

✔ Replacing a large amount of aquarium water (more than 40 percent) with freshly prepared saltwater. Because the new water lacks protective colloids (see page 39), the aquarium inhabitants are subjected to unnecessary stress.

✔ Undernourishment and poor diet.

✔ Stress from constant pursuit by predators.

✔ Toxins, for example, from injured sea cucumbers or decomposing corpses.

✔ Physiological stress factors, such as variations in temperature, pH, or salinity.

Diseases in Fish

The most common disease in marine fish is infestation with external parasites, some of which are visible on the fish's body during a particular developmental phase. The most familiar of these pathogens are *Amblyoodinium ocellatum* (coral reef disease) and *Cryptocaryon irritans* (white spot disease). Either will spread with alarming rapidity, because during their reproductive stage they move through the water like plankton and can infest all the fish in your aquarium.

Odinium parasites are minute protozoans. When colonizing the skin and fins, they are visible as a fine velvety coating on the fish's skin. Affected fish rub against rocks and coral. The parasites penetrate the gills, destroying tissue. A severe infestation leads to respiratory distress and suffocation.

Cryptocaryon parasites are considerably larger and result in milky-white spots, which are cyst-like lesions, on the fish's body and in the gills. The fish scrape against rocks and coral and show signs of respiratory distress. If heavily infested, a fish may die within four to five days after the first symptoms appear.

Both of these diseases are treated with a copper sulfate solution (sold in pet stores) in a "hospital" aquarium. Invertebrates and higher algae must not be exposed to the copper. Copper is very toxic. When using it, check the level every day. Because poor water quality is often a contributing factor to both diseases, you should also take the following measures:

✔ Clean the mechanical filters.

✔ Adjust protein skimmers to the highest setting.

✔ Many experienced aquarists recommend replacing the aquarium water with "aged" seawater.

✔ To improve hygiene conditions, add preparations containing potassium permanganate or other strong oxidizing agents (sold in pet stores). These can be used in aquariums containing algae and invertebrates.

✔ Increasing the water temperature to 84°F (29°C) and turning off the lights for two days also reduces the number of parasites.

The Azure Damselfish and other damselfish are hardy species, resistant to disease.

Good water quality is essential for healthy fish and invertebrates.

In addition to these measures, there are other methods for improving the hygiene conditions in your aquarium. Any time your fish get sick, consult your retailer or an experienced marine aquarium hobbyist about appropriate treatment methods. Parasites are not the only potential problem; there are a great many bacterial, fungal, and viral infections, but these are less common, and often only a specialist will recognize them. All are treatable with preparations sold in pet stores.

Pest Infestations in Corals

Corals in an aquarium may fall prey to small snails and crustaceans. These parasites, which are about ¼ to ½ inch (5–10 mm) in size and often resemble their victims in color, are usually active at night. Affected corals show signs of being nibbled at. With practice, you can learn to identify these pests and remove them with tweezers.

Corals are also attacked by planarians, tiny (about ⅛ inch, 1–3 mm) red, green, or brownish flatworms. Dragonets are natural enemies of these worms. Often, simply removing the visible worms with a suction tube and introducing a pair of dragonets is enough to resolve the problem.

OBSERVING BEHAVIOR

If you take the time to watch the goings-on in your saltwater aquarium, you can learn a good deal about the fascinating behavior of fish and invertebrates, developed in the course of evolution as these creatures adapted to life in the coral reef.

Behavior of Fish

Territoriality: Many species of fish are decidedly territorial. They claim a particular area in the aquarium and chase off any intruder. Surgeonfish, such as the Yellow Tang, express this territorial claim by holding their dorsal fins erect. If another surgeonfish approaches too near, they raise the short scalpel-like spines near the base of the tail (the origin of their common name) and attack their rival fiercely. This can lead to serious injury.

Established anemonefish and blennies may even nip at the aquarium keeper's hand to emphasize their territorial claim.

Schooling: Perhaps the best-known protective maneuver of fish is their schooling behavior. Fish are safer when they travel in groups, because a predator has difficulty concentrating on a single fish. In the marine aquarium, you can see a vivid example of schooling in the damselfish, darting among the corals in platoons of four or five fish. A damselfish kept as

The symbiosis of anemones and anemonefish is but one of the many mini-communities in the tropical coral reef.

a single specimen will be more timid and apprehensive than its schooling counterparts.

Courtship and mating: The courtship, mating, spawning, and brood care of saltwater fish is fascinating—perhaps the most intriguing aspect of keeping a marine aquarium. Since the early 1990s, it has become increasingly possible to breed marine fish in captivity. To be sure, maintaining a pair over a long period is not always possible for every fish species. When circumstances permit, however, the aquarium hobbyist should certainly attempt to keep a pair.

Indeed, fish of certain species need a partner in order to live a "normal" life in the aquarium. These include some species of gobies and all anemonefish.

The sexual development of the Yellow Wrasse includes a very interesting feature. If you place two juveniles of equal size in the aquarium, one will develop into a male and the other into a female. The male, which can be recognized by green stripes on its head, also grows to be somewhat larger than the female.

The same phenomenon occurs in many other species of fish, promoting the survival of that species in the reef environment. When an older

TIP

Observing Your Fish

✔ For best results, sit quietly in front of the aquarium for at least 15 to 30 minutes. The fish need some time to grow accustomed to the presence of an observer. Keep in mind that the fish are just as aware of your busy comings and goings as you are of their activity within the aquarium.

✔ It can be very interesting to watch the aquarium in the nighttime hours, aided by a flashlight. Many animals become active only at night. Corals take on different interesting shapes. For example, they may draw themselves in to "sleep," or extend their tentacles to capture plankton. This is also a time when predators, such as the nudibranchs, bristleworms, and small crustaceans that munch on corals, are on the prowl. These pests are difficult to detect during the daytime, but if you spy them at night, it's a simple matter to collect and remove them.

fish has lost its mate, a juvenile can still develop as the appropriate sex. In some species, such as the anemonefish, a male can change into a female, although a female cannot change her sex.

In a pair of fairy basslets, the larger fish is usually the male. Therefore, it's often possible to form a pair by selecting one small and one larger fish. When the fish are ready to spawn, the male seeks out a cave and lines it with natural materials from the aquarium, such as algae, sponges, and small pebbles. If a suitable hollow is not available, the male will attempt to construct one from the available materials. The female deposits the eggs in the prepared hollow. When they hatch, the fry are very small. Transfer them to a separate aquarium with abundant plankton; if left in the main aquarium, they would soon be eaten.

When anemonefish are ready to spawn, the male prepares a smooth surface near the host anemone. The female attaches the eggs to this site, where the male fertilizes and tends them. Waving his fins, the male keeps a continuous stream of oxygen-rich water flowing past the clutch so that the eggs will not become moldy. If one egg dies, the male will pluck it out to protect the rest of the clutch (see page 55). The parents leave their eggs only briefly to eat, and they are quite aggressive in defending against intruders during the brooding period. It's best to leave them undisturbed, because they will even attack your hand if it comes too near. The brooding period ranges from 8 to 11 days, depending on the temperature and the species. The newly hatched fry must be raised in a separate aquarium. The main aquarium does not provide enough suitable food or sufficient protection against other animals. To successfully raise many marine fish species that regularly breed in aquariums, you must maintain cultures of marine rotifers and other microscopic foods. Starter cultures and instructions for their care are sold by specialty suppliers.

The reproductive behavior of seahorses is unusual. During courtship, the male swims about the female with his brood pouch enlarged. To mate, the male and female cling to each other with their flexible tails, and the female deposits her eggs in the male's pouch, where they are fertilized (see page 57). After about four weeks, the male gives birth to the tiny (up to 0.4 inch, 1 cm) live young. As with

other fish, the young seahorses must be raised in a separate aquarium.

A pair of Pink Skunk anemonefish stands guard over its eggs.

Behavior of Invertebrates

The "migration" of anemones: Certain species of sea anemones can change their location in the aquarium. This "migration" is usually an indication that the anemone's original site did not meet its needs, or that incompatibilities with other corals developed. To move, the anemone detaches its basal disk from the aquarium substrate and drifts with the current to a new site. Some symbiotic anemones will wander about the aquarium until they find the location that suits them best. Leather corals or soft corals placed in an unfavorable site cannot move about as the anemones do. Instead, they strive to grow towards better light, developing elongated "necks" and tentacles in the process. This is a signal to move them to a brighter area.

Propagation of corals: It's fascinating to consider the many and varied possibilities for the propagation of corals. Corals can reproduce sexually by sending out eggs and sperm cells, but this behavior is rarely observed and relatively little researched. However, healthy corals readily propagate in the aquarium by budding or division.

BEHAVIOR
GUIDE

You can make many interesting observations if you know how to interpret the behavior of your aquarium fish.

👉 *This is what my fish are doing.*

❓ *What does it mean?*

❗ *Here's what to do!*

👆 Large spot on the dorsal fin.

❓ The "eye spot" is defensive camouflage for the Marine Betta. It repels predators.

❗ The marking is normal.

👆 Gobies scoop sand into their mouths.

❓ They do this as they seek food.

❗ Be sure to provide fine coral sand in the aquarium for gobies.

👆 A hawkfish perches on a rock.

❓ It is waiting to pounce on its prey.

❗ Don't expect your hawkfish to swim around as freely as your other fish.

👆 Sea anemone withdraws into itself.

❓ It seeks protection from predators.

❗ Don't keep anemones with too many pygmy angelfish or other species that nip at them.

👁 Yellow Tangs with fins erect.

❓ Fierce defenders of territory.

❗ To avoid battles, it's best to keep only a single specimen.

☝ Cleaner Wrasse sways to and fro.

❓ This is how other fish identify it as a "cleaner."

❗ Watch how it plucks parasites from their bodies.

☝ Seahorses intertwine.

❓ They are mating. The female deposits her eggs in the male's brood pouch.

❗ Do not disturb them.

Seahorse with 👈 enlarged brood pouch.

This is a pregnant male. ❓

When the young ❗ emerge, raise them in a separate aquarium.

☝ Cleaner shrimp feels its way along a fish's body.

❓ It hunts for parasites on the skin and gills.

❗ This behavior benefits both shrimp and fish.

Cleaner Shrimp remove harmful parasites from fish.

For example, disc anemones form knob-like buds that separate from the basal disk to form new "daughter" anemones. Disc anemones can also propagate by division. In that case, as frequently seen in elephant-ear corals (*Metarhodactis sp.*), a second mouth opening gradually develops, until finally two new independent anemones are formed.

You can propagate your corals artificially by separating the polyps. To do this, cut, break, or tie off a section and move it to another site in the aquarium. Fasten it on or between rocks until the new coral has attached itself to the substrate. This simple method can be used successfully with leather corals and soft corals.

Propagation of starfish: Many starfish reproduce sexually by releasing eggs. In some cases, however, as in certain *Linckia* species

(the Blue Linckia is one), starfish also reproduce asexually. The starfish drops one or two of its arms, and each part regenerates to form a new entire specimen. However, Blue Linckia may spontaneously lose arms also when they are seriously ill.

Fish and Invertebrates Living Together

A multitude of intriguing behavior patterns have evolved among fish and invertebrates in the ecological community of the coral reef.

Fish use the coral not only as hiding places, but also to groom their skin. They remove external parasites by rubbing against the adhesive surfaces of the corals, or swim slowly past the coral polyps and allow them to devour the parasites.

Many corals also serve as food for fish. This is evident in the aquarium when the corals draw themselves partly or completely inward as certain fish species, such as the pygmy angelfish, nibble at the coral polyps. Many corals have developed defensive mechanisms against their predators. For example, when a carpet anemone is touched, it emits white, bitter-tasting threads that hang from its mouth opening. Predators encounter these threads and are repelled before they can eat the corals.

On the other hand, the marine aquarium also contains many relationships based on mutual benefit to both animals. For example, cleaner shrimp scour the skin and gills of many coral reef fish, removing parasites. They even clean inside the fish's mouth. Remarkably, the fish suspend their predatory activity and let the otherwise tasty shrimp finish their work unharmed. The Cleaner Wrasse (*Labroides dimidiatus*) also engages in this combined grooming and harvesting.

The best-known symbiotic relationship in the marine aquarium, however, is that of the sea anemones and the anemonefish of the genus *Amphiprion*. Dwelling among the stinging tentacles of their host anemones, the anemonefish find refuge from predators. After a brief acclimation period, the sea anemone venom also coats the fishes' skin, affording additional protection. For their part, the anemonefish protect their host against predators such as the angelfish and butterfly, which like to nibble on the tentacles of the sea anemones. The symbi-

otic anemones subsist primarily on the products of photosynthesis carried out by unicellular algae, known as zooxanthellae, that live within their tissues.

Sea anemones also feed on plankton that float past them in the water, as well as on small fish and crustaceans that they paralyze with the stinging cells on their tentacles. The anemonefish are not involved in providing food for the sea anemones, as was once thought. Rather, as the alert aquarium keeper will observe, sea anemones often are forced to share tidbits of food with the anemonefish. The anemonefish may transport a good-sized morsel to the anemone, but the host receives only the leftovers, after the anemonefish has eaten its fill.

Perched on a rock encrusted with button polyps and red algae, a Bicolor Blenny surveys its surroundings.

*Royal Gramma
(Gramma loreto).*

Organizations

Aquarium Frontiers Online
Internet address:
    http://www.aquariumfrontiers.com/default.asp

Canadian Society of Aquarium Clubs
95 East 31st Street
Hamilton, Ontario
L8V 3N9 Canada

Center for Marine Conservation
1725 De Sales Street, NW
Washington, D.C. 20036
Internet address: http://www.cmc-ocean.org

The Cousteau Society
870 Greenbriar Circle, Suite 402
Chesapeake, Virginia 23320-2641
e-mail address: cousteau@infi.net

Federation of American Aquarium Societies
Membership Information
4816 East 64th St.
Indianapolis, Indiana 46220-4828

Marine Aquarium Societies of North America
    (MASNA Conference)
P.O. Box 508
Penns Park, Pennsylvania 18943
Internet address: http://www.MASNA.org/

Books

Blasiola II, George C. *The New Saltwater Aquarium Handbook.* Hauppauge, New York: Barron's Educational Series, Inc., 1991.
Delbeek, J.C. and Julian Sprung. *The Reef Aquarium: A Comprehensive Guide to the Identification and Care of Tropical Marine Invertebrates, Volume 1.* Coconut Grove, Florida: Ricordea Publishing, Inc., 1997.
Fenner, Robert. *The Conscientious Marine Aquarist.* Shelburne, Vermont: Microcosm, 1998.
Goldstein, Robert. *Marine Reef Aquarium Handbook.* Hauppauge, New York: Barron's Educational Series, Inc., 1997.
Moe, Martin A., Jr. *Marine Aquarium Reference. Systems and Invertebrates.* Plantation, Florida: Green Turtle Publications, 1989.

Sprung, Julian, and J.C. Delbeek. *The Reef Aquarium: A Comprehensive Guide to the Identification and Care of Tropical Marine Invertebrates, Volume 2.* Coconut Grove, Florida: Ricordea Publishing, Inc., 1997.
Stadelmann, Peter. *Setting Up an Aquarium.* Hauppauge, New York: Barron's Educational Series, Inc., 2000.
Tullock, John H. *Your First Marine Aquarium.* Hauppauge, New York: Barron's Educational Series, Inc., 1998.
——. *Dictionary of Aquarium Terms.* Hauppauge, New York: Barron's Educational Series, Inc., 2000.

Periodicals

Aquarium Fish magazine
Fancy Publications, Inc.
P.O. Box 6050
Mission Viejo, California 92690

Freshwater and Marine Aquarium magazine
144 West Sierra Madre Boulevard
Sierra Madre, California 91024

Marine Fish Monthly
Publishing Concepts Corp.
3243 Highway 61 East
Lutrell, Tennessee 37779

Tropical Fish Hobbyist
TFH Publications, Inc.
One TFH Plaza
Neptune, New Jersey 07753

About the Author

Axel Tunze studied physical technology with a focus on technology and environmental protection. He also ran a marine aquarium specialty shop and is now the managing director of TUNZE Aquarientechnik GmbH.

About the Artist

Renate Holzner works as a freelance illustrator in Regensburg, Germany. Her broad repertoire ranges from line drawings to photorealistic illustrations and computer graphics.

Photography Credits

Angermeyer: pages 18 bottom left, 24 top left, 57 top right; Bilder Pur/Bavendam: page 15 top left; Bildur Pur/Gibbs/OSF: pages 18 top left, 34; Bilder Pur/Göthel: front cover (small photo); Bilder Pur/Hulse/Rainbow: page 23; Bilder Pur/Huss/Wildlife: page 8; Bilder Pur/Kerstitch/Global: back cover; Bilder Pur/NAS/Hall: pages 52, 55; Bilder Pur/NAS/McHugh: pages 56 top right, 57 bottom right; Bilder Pur/NAS/McConnaughey: page 25 top right; Bilder Pur/NAS/Myers: page 20; Bilder Pur/Tavernier/BIOS: pages 6–7, 14 top left; Bilder Pur/Westmorland/Global Pic: page 56 bottom center; blickwinkel/Aßmann: page 15 bottom right; blickwinkel/Göthel: pages 4–5, 19 top right, 24 center right, 25 bottom right; Kahl: pages 9, 10, 11, 13, 21, 24 top right, 24 bottom left, 36, 48, 49 (small photo), 50, 53, 57 bottom left, 64–inside back cover; König: pages 2–3, 14 center right, 18 center right, 19 top left, 25 center left, 27 right, 38, 56 center right, 59, 61; Lange/Angermayer: page 67 top left; Nieuwenhuizen: pages 22, 30, 33, 35; Schmidbauer: page 27 left; Schraml: pages 43, 51, 56 center left; Silvestris/Attken: page 25 top left; Silvestris/Fleetham: front cover (large photo), page 15 center left; Silvestris/Hecker: pages 15 top right, 58; Silvestris/Riepl: page 16; Silvestris/Weinzierl: inside front cover, pages 14 top left, 49 (large photo), 57 center right; Sprenat: pages 12, 19 center left, bottom right, 31, 42, 44; Tunze: page 18 top right; Verlag A.C.S./Brei: page 14 top right.

Important Note

Electrical equipment for the maintenance of aquariums is described in this book. Please be sure to observe the precautions given on page 32 and follow the manufacturer's instructions for installation and safe use.

Before you purchase a saltwater aquarium, check how much weight the floor can support in the location where you plan to set up the aquarium. Water damage resulting from broken glass, overflow, or leaks that develop in the tank cannot always be avoided.

Keep all fish medications and chemicals used to prepare the aquarium saltwater out of the reach of children.

Always wear gloves when handling sea anemones; otherwise, their stinging venom may cause injury to skin.

Acknowledgment

The author wishes to thank attorney Reinhard Hahn for contributions regarding legal matters, and Brigitte and Norbert Tunze for their assistance.

Photos on Book Cover, Title Page, Chapter Title Pages:

Front cover: Clown Anemonefish (*Amphiprion percula*) (large photo) and Orange Starfish (*Fromia monilis*) (small photo).
Back cover: Mandarin Fish (*Synchiropus splendidus*).
Page 1: Mandarin Fish.
Pages 2–3: Flame Angelfish (*Centropyge loriculus*).
Pages 4–5: Tropical coral reef.
Pages 6–7: Longnosed Hawkfish (*Oxycirrhites typus*).
Pages 64: Banded Hawkfish (*Cirrhitichthys falco*).

English translation © Copyright 2001 by Barron's Educational Series, Inc.

© 1999 by Gräfe und Unzer Verlag GmbH, Munich, Germany.

Original title of the book in German is *Meerwasser Aquarium*.

English translation by Celia Bohannon.

All inquiries should be addressed to:
Barron's Educational Series, Inc.
250 Wireless Boulevard
Hauppauge, NY 11788
http://www.barronseduc.com

International Standard Book No. 0-7641-1637-1

Library of Congress Catalog Card No. 00-104956

Printed in China

9 8 7 6 5 4

1 How do saltwater aquariums differ from freshwater aquariums?

Most saltwater aquariums contain not only fish, but a variety of invertebrates, such as corals, crustaceans, mollusks, and starfish.

2 Is a saltwater aquarium more expensive than a freshwater aquarium?

Yes. The average saltwater aquarium with a tank capacity of 80 gallons (300 L) can cost up to twice as much as a comparable freshwater aquarium.

3 Can I convert a freshwater aquarium to a saltwater aquarium?

Yes, if the tank is large enough. You will also need to add special equipment (such as protein skimmers) needed in a saltwater aquarium.

4 Will I be able to use some of the decorations from my freshwater aquarium?

Usually not. Saltwater aquariums are decorated with live rock (reef rock inhabited by algae, sponges, small crustaceans, and the like) and coral sand.

5 Why does a saltwater aquarium need so much light?

Corals live on energy obtained from light. Their tissues contain algae that supply the corals with oxygen and nutrients produced by photosynthesis.

Experts answer the ten most common questions about the saltwater aquarium.